WEEKEND GETAWAYS FROM

RICHMOND, VA

WRITTEN BY

JENNIFER TAYLOR CRAIG

LURAY

VIRGINIA BEACH

STAUNTON

CLIFTON FORGE

3-DAY

ESCAPES

UNDER

3 HOURS

AWAY

WEEKEND GETAWAYS FROM RICHMOND, VA -
3-DAY ESCAPES UNDER 3 HOURS AWAY

CONTENTS

SECTION 3: SEASONS & CELEBRATIONS   92

SECTION 4: PLANNING TOOLS & TRAVEL TIPS   102

PREFACE

I've spent much of my life planning getaways—first as an avid traveler, later as a vacation planner and writer focused on international travel, and more recently as the author of a new book series that celebrates the joy of staying closer to home. I've always held a personal belief that travel doesn't have to be grand to be meaningful.

Some of my favorite trips have been short, spontaneous, and just a couple hours down the road. They didn't require months of saving or complicated logistics—just a free weekend, a tank of gas, and a sense of adventure.

This book is a celebration of that shift in thinking. After years in the travel industry helping others plan their vacations, I wanted to create something that felt attainable, rewarding, and grounded in the realities of modern life. With economic uncertainty and all the challenges that come with busy schedules, our ability to take meaningful breaks has never felt more essential.

The destinations in this guide were chosen not only for their convenience, but for the way they can offer a new perspective in just a few short days. If you've ever felt the need for a quick escape but weren't sure where to go—I hope this book helps spark new ideas for your next great getaway.

INTRODUCTION
WELCOME TO THE WEEKEND GETAWAYS SERIES

Craving mountain air, a seaside walk, or just a break from the daily grind? This guide is your ticket to easy, memorable escapes. *Weekend Getaways from Richmond, VA* offers a curated mix of destinations—each chosen for its charm, character, and the kind of atmosphere that stays with you long after you return.

With over 15 years in travel and tourism, I've learned you don't need to cross an ocean or take weeks off to feel the reset that travel offers. A well-spent weekend can be just as refreshing. Maybe that means hiking into the woods with a packed cooler, sipping wine on a hillside, or slipping into a robe at a spa. You'll find ideas here to match your mood, your pace, and your budget.

Each entry highlights where to stay, what to eat, and what to do, with thoughtful tips to help you connect with the place—not just check it off a list. From hidden gems and scenic drives to splurge-worthy stays and great local meals, these destinations span the full spectrum of weekend adventures.

Virginia has always felt like the beginning of a good story—from misty Blue Ridge mornings to salt-air wandering along the coast—and I'm proud to call it home. This is the first edition in a growing series of guides designed to inspire quick, meaningful getaways from cities across the U.S.

For Richmond locals, VCU students, and visitors to the area, I hope this book encourages you to pack light, go somewhere new, and make the most of your weekends.

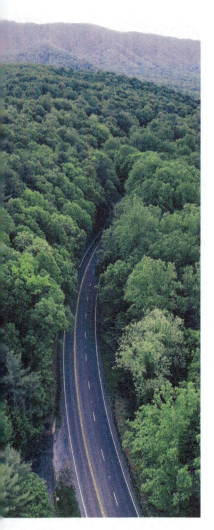

WHY WEEKEND TRAVEL MATTERS

Weekend travel is more than just a quick escape—it's a way to reset, reconnect, and rediscover joy in the everyday. In our increasingly connected, fast-paced world, we're more stressed and plugged in than ever before. Meanwhile, international travel has become more complicated and expensive, making those big overseas holidays harder to pull off.

But here's what I've learned after years in travel: you don't need to cross oceans to get the benefits that travel offers. Those dream vacations often leave you needing another vacation just to recover from all the logistics and over-packed itineraries. Weekend trips offer something different entirely. They give us permission to pause—to trade chores and routines for new landscapes and spontaneous moments. They help us stay curious, grounded, and inspired while keeping things simple.

And they're practical. A well-planned weekend getaway is cost-effective, low-stress, and easy to fit into real life. No asking for extended time off, no elaborate packing lists. Just you, a destination, and a little time carved out to live fully and travel well.

HOW TO USE THIS GUIDE

This book was made to keep your planning simple, your choices clear, and your weekends unforgettable. Each destination includes both budget and luxury options, so you can tailor your trip—or blend both for your perfect getaway.

Every entry follows the same format, making it easy to compare places at a glance. You'll find:

- When to Go – Seasonal highlights and ideal timing
- Why It's Worth the Trip – What makes it special
- What to Do – Activities, landmarks, and local gems
- Where to Stay & Eat – Options for every budget
- Explore More – Nearby towns and scenic detours to consider

Each getaway destination includes the distance from Richmond and is designed to be doable in a weekend—easy to reach, rewarding to experience.

While some businesses in this guide may come and go, the spirit of each trip remains. Use this book as a starting point. Follow a sample itinerary or take from it what inspires you most. The aim is to make travel feel possible—something you can turn to when you need a break. Not months from now, but now. This weekend.

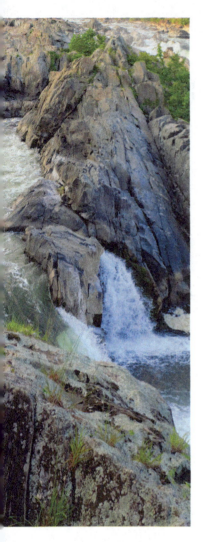

WHAT COUNTS AS A WEEKEND GETAWAY?

In this guide, a "weekend getaway" means exactly what it sounds like: a trip you can take from Friday to Sunday (or maybe Monday, if you stretch it). We've focused on destinations that are reachable within a couple of hours of Richmond by car or train—far enough to feel like a true escape, but close enough that you won't spend all your time traveling.

This isn't about cramming a complete vacation into a couple of days—it's about creating space for joy, connection, and curiosity in the time you do have. We've included a mix of tried-and-true favorites and under-the-radar finds, each with something special to offer. You don't need a passport, weeks of planning, or a packed suitcase. Just pick a place, grab a friend (or go solo!), and go see something new.

When you're craving a glorious beach sunrise, a refreshing mountain hike, or a cozy B&B, the destinations and recommendations in this book have been selected to satisfy those urges.

Let this guide live in your glovebox, your weekend bag, or on your bedside table. Whenever the itch to escape strikes, you'll have inspiration at the ready—no long planning process required.

SECTION 1.

PLANNING YOUR PERFECT ESCAPE

A great getaway doesn't require a huge budget, a packed itinerary, or months of planning. What it does require is a little clarity about what kind of weekend you want, how much time you have, and what's going to make it feel truly worthwhile. This section helps you lay that foundation.

We'll begin with what to pack, what to leave behind, and a few small habits that can make weekend travel smoother, lighter, and more enjoyable from start to finish.

From there, we'll cover some practical guidance for shaping a trip around your needs. Maybe you want to rest, recharge, reconnect, or simply change your surroundings. No matter your reason, choosing a destination that fits your life right now makes all the difference.

You'll also find an overview of transportation options: road trips, regional trains, and short-haul flights, so you can pick the route that makes the most sense for your pace, your budget, and your preferences. Taken together, these tips are meant to cut down the stress, remove the guesswork, and help you get out the door feeling ready, not rushed.

PACKING TIPS FOR WEEKEND WARRIORS

A weekend trip calls for a light touch. You don't need to pack like you're heading abroad for two weeks. The goal is to travel light, stay nimble, and still feel prepared for whatever your weekend brings. A smaller bag means less stress, fewer decisions, and more freedom once you arrive.

Start with a compact weekender bag or backpack. Prioritize clothing that mixes and matches easily, and always check the forecast. Virginia and the surrounding region can throw you a curveball. Layers are your friend. And don't forget one "elevated" outfit, just in case your plans take a turn for the fancy.

Toiletries? Go mini. Shoes? One pair for walking, one for style if needed. Tech? Keep it simple. Chargers, headphones, and maybe a backup battery. You're getting away, not relocating.

The beauty of weekend travel is how little you actually need. A few well-chosen essentials, a flexible mindset, and you're out the door.

FINDING YOUR TRAVEL STYLE

One of the best things about weekend travel is that it can be whatever you need it to be. Maybe this is the weekend you watch the sunrise from a tent, sip coffee on a porch swing, and keep your wallet mostly closed. Or maybe it's the weekend for champagne brunch, a luxury spa, and sleeping in crisp white sheets with room service on standby. Either way—you're doing it right.

In this guide, we highlight both budget and luxury options for each destination. That means you can decide what works for your life right now, and even blend the two.

Want to splurge on a beautiful boutique hotel but keep meals casual? Go for it. Prefer to save on lodging so you can book a guided kayak tour or dinner at that place with the tasting menu? We've got you.

This isn't about one being better than the other—it's about making the most of your time and your money, wherever you are. No matter your pace, your preferences, or your priorities, there's room here to do it your way.

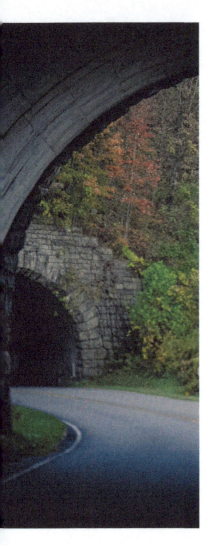

TRANSPORTATION FROM RICHMOND

One of the best things about Richmond is how well-connected it is. From the mountains to the coast to nearby towns, there are multiple ways to get where you're going. This section gives you an overview of your transportation options so you can choose what fits your schedule, your budget, and your style of travel.

Driving is often the simplest and most flexible way to explore weekend destinations from Richmond. With several major highways intersecting the city, road trips are both straightforward and scenic. You're often just a couple of hours from a whole new experience.

Prefer to skip the car? Richmond also offers easy access to regional trains, intercity buses, and short-haul flights that let you cover more ground with less stress—ideal for travelers who'd rather relax and enjoy the ride than drive.

No matter how you get there, this section will help you choose the best route and plan accordingly—so you can spend less time figuring things out and more time enjoying your weekend.

DRIVING ROUTES

If you've got a car (or can borrow one), Richmond is a springboard for memorable road trips. Take I-64 west to the mountains, I-95 north toward history and culture, or head east to the coast. The drive is often part of the pleasure.

All of the destinations in this book are within a 1–3 hour radius of the city, giving you flexibility. For something slow and winding, try the Blue Ridge Parkway. For efficiency and directness, major interstates make it easy to reach other cities, mountain towns, or the beachfront without the guesswork.

If you have time to spare, consider taking the longer route now and then. Back roads, byways, and small-town stops can turn a simple drive into part of the adventure. Sometimes the best memories come from detours you didn't plan.

Before you go, check for tolls, construction, and seasonal detours, especially during peak foliage or summer weekends. A little pre-trip navigation can save you time and maybe even show you something unexpected along the way. Pair your playlist, pack some snacks, and hit the road. The route is half the fun.

TRAIN & BUS OPTIONS

If you'd rather not drive or just want to relax while someone else handles the road, Richmond has reliable train and bus service that makes getting away simple. With multiple departures and convenient stations, it's easy to swap traffic for a window seat. Amtrak runs daily routes from both Main Street Station and Staples Mill to places like Washington, D.C., Charlottesville, or Raleigh. With roomy seats, Wi-Fi, and views along the way, it's a relaxed way to start your weekend.

Bus service has also improved in recent years. Options like Megabus, Greyhound, and Virginia Breeze connect Richmond to a wide range of destinations at budget-friendly prices. These services work well when you want to travel light and keep costs down. These options give you the freedom to skip the car and still enjoy a full weekend escape. Just grab your ticket, pack light, and enjoy the ride.

Trains and buses also drop you right into the heart of many destinations. No parking, no navigating, just more time to wander and discover.

REGIONAL
FLIGHTS

While all the destinations in this book are easily reached by car or train, it's worth remembering that Richmond International Airport (RIC) also makes quick weekend flights a viable option for future getaways. Cities like Charlotte, Asheville, and even New York can be reached in under two hours by air, offering a faster, often less stressful alternative to long drives. As budget carriers and regional routes grow, flying can sometimes rival the cost of gas and parking. If you decide to fly, early departures and late returns help maximize your time away. With a carry-on bag and a little planning, even a whirlwind trip can feel like a true escape.

So while you won't need a plane for the places in this guide, keep RIC in mind. It's a great launchpad for expanding your weekend horizons later on.

Weekend travel doesn't have to follow one formula. Some trips call for the ease of a familiar route, others for the adventure of trying something entirely new. When you're ready to plan your next getaway, consider all the options. The key is choosing what fits your schedule and energy level that particular weekend.

TRAVEL TOOLS & APPS

Smart travel doesn't mean complicated travel. It means using the right tools to simplify and enhance your trip. Planning a last-minute escape or coordinating a multi-stop itinerary, these apps and resources can save time, money, and stress while helping you travel with more confidence.

- Google Maps for directions, food spots, and traffic updates.
- Roadtrippers finds scenic routes and quirky roadside stops.
- GasBuddy shows the cheapest gas near you.
- Rome2Rio compares options across car, bus, train, or flight.
- Use Amtrak and airline apps for mobile tickets and alerts.
- HotelTonight and Airbnb offer last-minute lodging deals.
- OpenTable and Resy make booking restaurant tables easy.
- PackPoint creates packing lists based on weather and activities.

Before your trip, download the apps you plan to use and set up accounts in advance. A little prep now saves time later, and the fewer things you have to think about while you're traveling, the more time you'll have to enjoy the journey.

SECTION 2.

GETAWAYS BY DESTINATION

This is where the planning gets practical. Each destination in this section is presented in a clear, consistent format to make planning simple and stress-free.

You'll start with a quick snapshot: how far it is from Richmond, the local geography, the best times to visit, and what kind of vibe to expect, followed by a short summary of why the trip is worth taking. These overviews help you quickly gauge which getaways fit your style, interests, and timing.

From there, you'll discover nearby places to explore, smart transportation tips, and a curated list of top things to do. These suggestions reflect not just what's popular, but what's genuinely worth your time. Browse local highlights chosen to help you experience each place with depth and ease.

The second half of each entry focuses on personalized planning. You'll find two weekend outlines: one for budget-friendly travel and one for a more luxurious stay, each with suggestions for where to sleep, what to eat, and how to spend your time. Use them as-is, as inspiration, mix and match, or build something entirely your own. When you're planning a trip with a new flame, catching up with an old friend, or seeking a solo escape to reset, this section will help you spot opportunities and save time.

QUICK TRIPS

WILLIAMSBURG

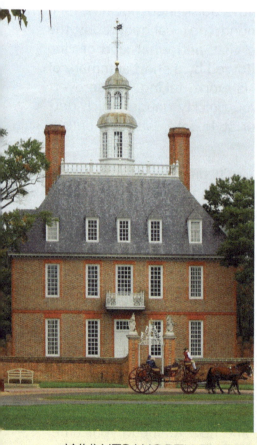

DISTANCE FROM RVA

1 hour by car or train

GEOGRAPHY

SE Virginia, part of the Historic Triangle with Jamestown and Yorktown

BEST TIME TO VISIT

Spring, fall, and December festivals

GENERAL VIBE

Historic, charming, and flexible—perfect for families, couples, or curious solo travelers.

WHY ITS WORTH THE TRIP

Williamsburg mixes centuries-old history with contemporary comforts. Wander the cobblestone streets of Colonial Williamsburg, enjoy craft brews at local pubs, or unwind at a luxury spa. Whether you're here for the past or the present, it's a weekend getaway that balances culture, relaxation, and fun.

EXPLORE MORE

YORKTOWN, VA | 20 MIN. E

This waterfront town offers American Revolution history, a scenic beach walk, and a charming riverfront promenade lined with shops and cafes. Don't miss sunset views from the Riverwalk or fishing pier.

JAMESTOWN, VA | 15 MIN. SW

Explore the original 1607 settlement at Historic Jamestowne or dive into immersive exhibits at the Jamestown Settlement museum. Costumed interpreters and replica ships bring early America vividly to life.

NEW KENT COUNTY, VA | 30 MIN. NE

Known for wineries, horse farms, and scenic drives—perfect for a relaxed afternoon sipping wine in the countryside. Visit a vineyard tasting room or stop by a roadside farm stand.

TIPS

Reach Williamsburg in about 1 hour via I-64 E. The town also has an Amtrak station with direct service from Richmond, making it a great pick for a train-based getaway. Most of the historic core and downtown are walkable.

WILLIAMSBURG

THINGS TO DO

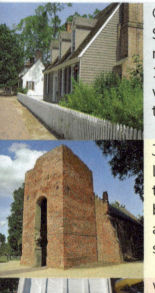

COLONIAL WILLIAMSBURG
Step back in time in this immersive living-history museum where costumed interpreters bring the 18th century to life. Explore historic buildings, watch traditional trades in action, and chat with townsfolk about daily life and the revolution.

JAMESTOWNE SETTLEMENT
Located near the site of the original 1607 colony, this museum explores the clash and cooperation between early English settlers, Powhatan Indians, and African peoples. Climb aboard replica ships and wander through reconstructed forts.

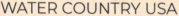

WATER COUNTRY USA
Cool off at this expansive water park, perfect for families or thrill-seekers. With wave pools, water coasters, and lazy rivers, it's a great way to spend a sunny summer day.

TIPS

- Visit during Grand Illumination (December)
- Rent a paddleboat at Waller Mill Park
- Ride the Jamestown-Scotland Ferry
- Explore the Virginia Musical Museum

THINGS TO DO

BUSCH GARDENS WILLIAMSBURG
A European-themed amusement park that blends high-speed coasters with top-notch shows, lush landscaping, and food from across the continent. It's consistently rated as one of the most beautiful theme parks in the country.

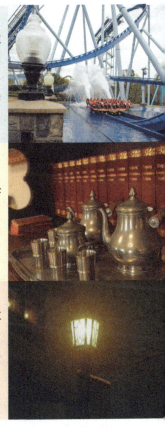

WILLIAMSBURG ANTIQUE MALL
A treasure trove for vintage lovers and collectors, this enormous space houses dozens of well-organized booths featuring everything from mid-century furniture and decor to Civil War-era relics and fine china.

GHOST TOURS
As night falls, join one of the city's famous ghost tours through the historic district. With dim lanterns lighting the way, guides share chilling tales rooted in local legend and historical fact—an atmospheric way to end your day.

TIPS

- Walk Among the Giant President Heads
- Stroll the Williamsburg Botanical Garden
- Treat Yourself at Wythe Candy & Gourmet Shop
- Play Retro Games at Ripley's Arcade

WILLIAMSBURG

BUDGET TRAVEL

WHERE TO STAY

Stay at one of the affordable motels along Richmond Road or book a simple Airbnb close to Colonial Williamsburg. You won't have trouble finding rooms under $100 a night, especially if you book a few weeks ahead. It's a great area for walkability and easy access to the historic district.

WHAT TO EAT

Start your day with coffee and breakfast at Aromas or Shorty's Diner, then swing by The Cheese Shop for a classic sandwich and house dressing. For dinner, try Food for Thought or Rick's Cheesesteak Shop. Don't skip dessert—The Meadows Custard is a local favorite.

SAMPLE ITINERARY

- Friday: Check in, grab dinner, and end the night with a ghost tour.

- Saturday: Explore Colonial history, browse Merchants Square, and enjoy custard before dinner.

- Sunday: Morning coffee, hearty breakfast, one last museum visit, then head home.

LUXURY TRAVEL

WHERE TO STAY

Book a suite at the Williamsburg Inn, Kingsmill Resort, or a high-end B&B with spa access. For a stay with historic flair, try the Colonial Houses—an official Colonial Williamsburg hotel with 18th-century charm and modern comfort. Many luxury stays also offer golf, fine dining, and curated guest experiences.

WHAT TO EAT

Dine at Fat Canary or Amber Ox for upscale Southern cuisine with a modern twist. Enjoy tasting flights at the Williamsburg Winery, or savor refined dishes at Cochon on 2nd or Rockafellers. Many restaurants feature seasonal menus with locally sourced ingredients and award-winning wine lists.

SAMPLE ITINERARY

• Friday: Settle in and enjoy wine and dinner downtown.

• Saturday: Book a carriage ride, tour historic sites, relax with spa time, and enjoy a chef's table dinner.

• Sunday: Savor a gourmet brunch, then stroll through botanical gardens or winery grounds.

CHARLOTTESVILLE

DISTANCE FROM RVA

1 hour 15 minutes by car

GEOGRAPHY

Central Virginia, at the foothills of the Blue Ridge Mountains

BEST TIME TO VISIT

Spring for blooms, fall for foliage and wine festivals

GENERAL VIBE

Sophisticated yet relaxed, outdoorsy with a touch of indulgence—ideal for couples, food lovers, and weekend wanderers.

WHY ITS WORTH THE TRIP

Charlottesville blends history, hospitality, and natural beauty at the edge of the Blue Ridge Mountains. Spend your morning exploring Jefferson's legacy, your afternoon sipping wine on a hillside, and your evening enjoying live music downtown. With its mix of small-town charm and elevated experiences, it's the kind of place that invites you to linger.

EXPLORE MORE

CROZET, VA | 25 MIN. W

A charming small town with craft breweries, farm-to-table restaurants, and mountain views. Don't miss a pint at Pro Re Nata. Explore the Crozet Tunnel Greenway—a restored 19th-century railroad tunnel turned walking trail.

KESWICK, VA | 15 MIN. E

Known for its rolling countryside and winding drives, this is a great place for wine tasting or a peaceful stop en route to Monticello. Don't miss Keswick Vineyards or a leisurely drive along Route 231, one of Virginia's most beautiful byways.

BARBOURSVILLE, VA | 30 MIN. NE

Visit Barboursville Vineyards and the historic ruins for a mix of wine and history in a pastoral setting. Explore the nearby Four County Players Theater or take a country drive past historic estates and farmland dotted with old stone fences.

TIPS

Charlottesville is about 1 hour and 15 minutes west of Richmond by car via I-64. You can also take the Northeast Regional train from Main Street Station, with two daily departures and a travel time of about 3 hours. Once there, it's easy to get around by foot, rideshare, or taxi.

CHARLOTTESVILLE
THINGS TO DO

MONTICELLO

Tour Thomas Jefferson's beautifully preserved plantation home and gardens. Rich in history and architecture, Monticello offers guided tours that explore Jefferson's legacy, inventions, and the design of this iconic estate.

HISTORIC DOWNTOWN MALL

One of the longest pedestrian malls in the country, this lively strip of restored buildings is home to boutiques, cafés, galleries, and live music venues. It's a perfect spot to stroll, shop, or grab a drink on a warm evening.

SAUNDERS-MONTICELLO TRAIL

This serene, well-maintained trail system is a favorite among locals for walking and running. It winds through lush woodlands and offers beautiful views—especially striking in the fall.

TIPS

- View local art at IX Art Park and the adjoining galleries
- Tour the Lewis & Clark keel-boat replica
- Tour the Fralin Museum of Art at UVA
- Book a goat snuggle session at Caromont Farm

THINGS TO DO

CARTER MOUNTAIN ORCHARD
Just outside town, this hilltop orchard is known for its seasonal fruit picking, homemade apple cider donuts, and sunset views. Visit in autumn for apple picking or spring for peaches and flowers.

UNLOCKED HISTORY ESCAPE ROOMS
With locally inspired puzzles and storytelling, this escape room experience is both fun and immersive. Great for couples, families, or groups of friends looking for a unique rainy-day activity.

BROWSE LOW OR HEYDAY ANTIQUES
Vintage lovers should stop by these standout shops. Low specializes in vintage clothing, vinyl records, and antiques with a rock 'n' roll edge, while Heyday offers a more curated collection of retro homewares and curios.

TIPS

- Visit the Saturday City Market for local goods
- Drive Route 151 for mountain-view breweries
- Catch sunset and cider at Carter Mountain
- Take a ghost tour downtown after dark

CHARLOTTESVILLE
BUDGET TRAVEL

WHERE TO STAY

Book a cozy Airbnb near historic Belmont or the UVA campus. Budget-friendly picks like The English Inn, Oakhurst Inn, or a one-bedroom suite at the Belmont Farmhouse offer charm, comfort, and great weekend rates. Many are walkable to coffee shops, breweries, and some of Charlottesville's best bites.

WHAT TO EAT

Grab breakfast at Bodo's Bagels, enjoy tacos from Brazos Tacos, and try a casual dinner at Citizen Burger Bar. For budget-friendly flavor with a local twist, check out Mockingbird's Southern comfort food, Caribbean plates at Pearl Island, or the always-reliable El Tio for classic Mexican. Plenty of food trucks and breweries also serve great options.

SAMPLE ITINERARY

- Friday: Check in and walk the Downtown Mall. Grab dinner and people-watch.

- Saturday: Explore UVA, visit the IX Art Park, then catch live music at a brewery.

- Sunday: Morning hike and bagels, then head home with a coffee to-go.

LUXURY TRAVEL

WHERE TO STAY

Treat yourself to a stay at The Clifton or Arcady Vineyard Bed and Breakfast—both offer elegant amenities, scenic grounds, and a peaceful setting. The Inn at Court Square blends historic charm with modern comfort right in downtown Charlottesville. For a truly elevated stay, Keswick Hall delivers top-tier luxury with sweeping countryside views.

WHAT TO EAT

Dine at The Ivy Inn or C&O for a culinary experience rooted in local flavor. For upscale steak and cocktails, try Black Cow Chophouse. Marigold at Keswick offers a picturesque, ingredient-driven menu, while Dr. Ho's Humble Pie serves elevated comfort food with chef cred. For wine tastings, head to Pippin Hill or Veritas Vineyards.

SAMPLE ITINERARY

- Friday: Settle into your inn and enjoy a sunset wine tasting.

- Saturday: Tour Monticello, followed by spa treatments and fine dining.

- Sunday: Brunch and a vineyard visit before the drive back.

QUICK TRIPS
SHENANDOAH

DISTANCE FROM RVA

1 hr 30 min by car

GEOGRAPHY

Western Virginia along the crest of the Blue Ridge Mountains

BEST TIME TO VISIT

Fall for colors, spring and summer for waterfalls

GENERAL VIBE

Expansive, peaceful, and wild—perfect for hikers, photographers, stargazers, and anyone in need of a mountain reset.

WHY ITS WORTH THE TRIP

With sweeping vistas, cascading waterfalls, and over 500 miles of trails, Shenandoah National Park is Virginia's most iconic outdoor escape. Drive Skyline Drive, hike to a summit, or spot deer in a misty meadow—the park's high-elevation landscapes offer a restorative sense of space and awe. You don't have to be a serious hiker to enjoy it. Just roll down the window or stop at an overlook.

EXPLORE MORE

WAYNESBORO, VA | 5 MIN. E

Just outside the Rockfish Gap Entrance, Waynesboro is a relaxed gateway town with Appalachian Trail access, the South River Greenway, and casual restaurants. It's a smart stop for supplies, a meal, or a riverside stroll.

AFTON, VA | 5 MIN. SE

Known for its mountain views and craft beverage trail, Afton offers wineries, breweries, and hikes like the Blue Ridge Tunnel—all just minutes from the Rockfish Gap entrance. A perfect blend of nature and local flavor.

STAUNTON, VA | 20 MIN. W

A vibrant small city with historic architecture, farm-to-table dining, and charming lodging options. Staunton is perfect for visitors who want to blend nature and culture in one weekend.

TIPS

Rockfish Gap is the closest entrance from Richmond and connects directly to the southern end of Skyline Drive. A vehicle is recommended, as overlooks are spaced out and there's no public transit. Other entrances like Swift Run, Thornton Gap, and Front Royal may suit travelers coming from elsewhere.

SHENANDOAH

THINGS TO DO

SKYLINE DRIVE
This scenic byway runs the length of the park and is its most famous feature. With 75 over-looks, it's perfect for a slow drive with plenty of photo stops—especially during peak foliage in October.

HUMPBACK ROCKS
Humpback Rocks is a steep 1-mile hike just out-side the park near Rockfish Gap, with sweeping views of the Shenandoah Valley. The trailhead is at milepost 5.8 on the Blue Ridge Parkway.

DOYLES RIVER FALLS
This moderate hike leads to two waterfalls—28 and 63 feet tall—with options for a short out-and-back or a longer loop via the Jones Run Trail. Trailhead is at milepost 81.1 on Skyline Drive.

TIPS

- Check the park's site for closures and permit updates
- Cell service is limited—bring a map or download ahead
- Short trails often have the best views - don't skip them
- In fall, arrive early to avoid Skyline Drive traffic

THINGS TO DO

WILDLIFE VIEWING

Look for deer, black bears, and wild turkeys, particularly around dawn and dusk. Less-trafficked trails like Limberlost are great for peaceful wildlife sightings.

VISITOR CENTERS & RANGER PROGRAMS

For more than maps, visit the Loft Mountain area near milepost 79.5. It's the closest stop from Rockfish Gap with trail info, seasonal ranger talks, and basic services.

CAMPING & STARGAZING

Camp at Loft Mountain and enjoy some of the darkest skies in Virginia. On clear nights, you'll spot stars, constellations, and even the Milky Way stretching overhead.

TIPS

- Store food properly and keep your distance from wildlife
- Weather shifts fast—bring layers and rain gear
- Loft Mountain Wayside has snacks, maps, and basics
- Stay on trail—shortcuts harm habitat and risk injury

SHENANDOAH

BUDGET TRAVEL

WHERE TO STAY

Camp at Loft Mountain Campground, located off Skyline Drive and easily accessible from Rockfish Gap. If you prefer to stay in town, Waynesboro offers affordable motels and cabin rentals, while Staunton has budget-friendly inns and B&Bs just a short drive away.

WHAT TO EAT

Bring picnic supplies or trail snacks from home, or stop at the seasonal Waynesboro Farmers Market before heading into the park. For a sit-down meal, grab a sandwich at Taste of Cuba in Waynesboro or enjoy flavorful curries at Taste of India in Staunton.

SAMPLE ITINERARY

- Friday: Arrive at Rockfish Gap, camp at Loft Mountain, and enjoy sunset from an overlook.

- Saturday: Morning hike to Doyles River Falls, picnic lunch, and dinner at Taste of Cuba in Waynesboro.

- Sunday: Sunrise drive along Skyline Drive, coffee at Crucible in Staunton, then head home.

LUXURY TRAVEL

WHERE TO STAY

Book a mountain-view cabin near Rockfish Gap, or opt for a refined stay at the Iris Inn or the stylish Maude & the Bear in Staunton—both offer upscale comfort and easy access to the park and nearby dining.

WHAT TO EAT

Start your day with brunch at Reunion Bakery & Espresso in Staunton, then wind down with dinner at Zynodoa or a reservation at Maude & the Bear. In the afternoon, enjoy a wine tasting at Barren Ridge or Veritas Vineyards.

SAMPLE ITINERARY

- Friday: Arrive in Staunton, check into your hotel, and enjoy dinner at Zynodoa.

- Saturday: Morning hike and picnic in Shenandoah, wine tasting in the afternoon, and sunset from Skyline Drive.

- Sunday: Brunch downtown, then a relaxed scenic drive home.

QUICK TRIPS
STAUNTON

DISTANCE FROM RVA
1 hour 40 min by car

GEOGRAPHY
Shenandoah Valley, just off I-81 and Skyline Drive

BEST TIME TO VISIT
Spring, fall, or December for holidays.

GENERAL VIBE
Classic, cultured, and a little quirky—great for foodies, theater lovers, and weekend wanderers.

WHY ITS WORTH THE TRIP

Staunton is one of Virginia's best-kept secrets—a walkable, artsy mountain town that blends historic architecture with unexpected creativity. With its charming downtown, Shakespeare theater, and local food scene, it's a town that punches well above its weight for culture and character.

EXPLORE MORE

WAYNESBORO, VA | 20 MIN. E

Waynesboro offers access to the Blue Ridge Parkway, Skyline Drive, and picturesque walks along the South River Greenway. A craft beer scene and local art spaces make it a relaxed stop for hikers, beer lovers, and those looking to unwind.

CHURCHVILLE, VA | 15 MIN. W

A quiet rural stop with scenic drives, especially beautiful in fall. Nearby Natural Chimneys Park features towering limestone formations and picnic areas, making it a worthwhile detour for those exploring the Shenandoah Valley.

MOUNT SIDNEY, VA | 25 MIN. N

This small village is known for its well-preserved 19th-century architecture and quiet charm. A peaceful place for a short drive, it's ideal for those who appreciate historic homes, country roads, and a slower pace.

TIPS

Reach Staunton in about 1 hour and 40 minutes via I-64 W. It's a straightforward drive and Amtrak also offers service to Staunton from Richmond. Once downtown, the town is compact and walkable with a charming historic district.

STAUNTON

THINGS TO DO

FRONTIER CULTURE MUSEUM

Travel through time at this open-air living history museum, which brings to life the daily experiences of early American settlers. Explore working farms, costumed interpreters, and hands-on activities for all ages.

GYPSY HILL PARK

A beloved community space with 200 acres of open green, Gypsy Hill offers walking trails, a duck pond, playgrounds, and even a small golf course. In the summer, catch live music at the bandstand or hop on the mini train.

HORSEBACK RIDING TOURS

Saddle up and take in the Shenandoah Valley from horseback with local guided tours that cater to both beginners and experienced riders. It's a relaxing and memorable way to explore the area's countryside.

TIPS

- Spot Sears kit-homes tucked in historic neighborhoods
- Grab a scoop at The Split Banana for handmade gelato
- Dragon's Hoard is packed with games and RPG gear
- Take the wooded walk to the overlook at Betsy Bell Park

THINGS TO DO

ANTIQUING IN DOWNTOWN STAUNTON
Staunton is perfect for antique lovers. Spend an afternoon browsing shops like 17 E Beverley Antiques and Staunton Antiques Center, both packed with treasures from vintage homewares to quirky collectibles and estate jewelry.

STAUNTON FARMERS MARKET
Held downtown on weekends during the warmer months, this vibrant market features fresh produce, local meats, baked goods, and handmade crafts. It's a great way to start your morning and support local artisans and farmers.

CIDERS FROM MARS
This modern cidery offers complex, creative hard ciders made from Virginia-grown apples. Their industrial-chic tasting room is a great stop for a casual afternoon drink, and flights let you sample a variety of flavors.

TIPS

- Tour the Woodrow Wilson Library and Museum
- Montgomery Hall Park has trails and disc golf
- Visit Blackfriars Theatre, a replica of a 1600s playhouse
- Downtown parking is free evenings and weekends

STAUNTON

BUDGET TRAVEL

WHERE TO STAY

Staunton has plenty of stays under $100, especially just outside the historic district where prices drop without sacrificing comfort. Even motels closer to downtown offer solid value, convenient access, and a chance to spend more on food, shopping, or catching a show. It's an easy place to plan a budget-friendly weekend.

WHAT TO EAT

Staunton has no shortage of great food at casual prices. Try pupusas at Gloria's, a burger from Remedy, or bold flavors at Thai Staunton. Chicano Boy is a local burrito and taco favorite, Pizza Luca serves crisp, wood-fired pies, and Wright's Dairy-Rite delivers retro drive-in charm with shakes and sandwiches.

SAMPLE ITINERARY

• Friday: Arrive and stroll downtown, then grab dinner at a local favorite, drinks at Ciders from Mars.

• Saturday: Visit museums, browse shops, hike Betsy Bell, and catch a show at Blackfriars.

• Sunday: Sip coffee, feed the ducks at Gypsy Hill Park, and head home refreshed.

LUXURY TRAVEL

WHERE TO STAY

For a refined stay, consider Berkeley Place or The Inn at Oakdene for historic elegance, spacious rooms, and serene settings. Hotel 24 South and The Frederick House offer boutique comfort with local charm, walkable access to downtown, and personalized service that adds to the experience.

WHAT TO EAT

Dine at Zynodoa for refined Southern farm-to-table or Edelweiss for cozy, traditional German fare. Sip craft cocktails and curated wines at The Green Room, or enjoy a relaxed tasting of Shenandoah Valley vintages at Ox-Eye Vineyards. For a full evening out, pair dinner with a show at nearby Blackfriars.

SAMPLE ITINERARY

• Friday: Check in, grab a massage at a local spa. Dinner at Zynodoa, drinks at Green Room.

• Saturday: Sleep in, go horseback riding at Star B Stables, enjoy a wine tasting at Barren Ridge, and catch a show at Blackfriars.

• Sunday: Savor brunch, then take a relaxing drive along Skyline Drive before heading home.

QUICK TRIPS

APPALACHIAN TRAIL

DISTANCE FROM RVA

1 hr 45 min by car

GEOGRAPHY

Blue Ridge Mountains and wooded ridgelines across central Virginia

BEST TIME TO VISIT

Fall for colors, spring for wildflowers

GENERAL VIBE

Peaceful and grounding, with just the right mix of solitude and scenery.

WHY ITS WORTH THE TRIP

The Appalachian Trail is a quiet giant—cutting through Virginia's mountains with timeless rhythm and unexpected accessibility. Enter at Swift Run Gap and you're stepping into Shenandoah National Park's middle corridor, where forested ridges, granite outcrops, and fog-draped overlooks offer a dose of wilderness less than two hours from Richmond. You don't need to go far to feel far away.

EXPLORE MORE

HARRISONBURG, VA | 30 MIN. W

A lively college town with a walkable downtown, great coffee shops, and a strong local food scene. Home to James Madison University, it's a great place to refuel with a sit-down meal, grab gear at a local outfitter, or spend the night in comfort.

GORDONSVILLE, VA | 30 MIN. SE

This historic crossroads town blends small-town charm with creative energy. Browse vintage shops, check out local art, and grab a Hot and Messy burger with fries and a Home Run Hefe at Patch Brewing Co.—a community favorite.

BARBOURSVILLE, VA | 35 MIN. S

Best known for its winery and the ruins of a Jefferson-designed mansion, Barboursville blends scenic vineyards with a touch of history. Book a tasting, linger over lunch at Palladio Restaurant, or enjoy the countryside from a quiet picnic spot.

TIPS

Driving is essential. Swift Run Gap is the most direct access from Richmond via Route 33 and offers a great mid-park starting point. Other options include Rockfish Gap near Staunton, Thornton Gap near Luray, and Front Royal to the north. For hikes outside the park, try Bear's Den by Middleburg or Dragon's Tooth by Roanoke.

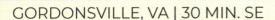

APPALACHIAN TRAIL

THINGS TO DO

HIGHTOP SUMMIT
A 3-mile round-trip hike from Swift Run Gap leads to one of the park's most underrated vistas. It's a moderate climb, but worth every step—especially at sunrise or during fall color. Quiet and less crowded than better-known peaks.

SOUTH RIVER FALLS TRAIL
This 4.6-mile out-and-back hike winds down to Shenandoah's third-highest waterfall. You'll pass wildflowers in spring, dense woods in summer, and cool mist at the falls year-round. Pack a lunch and linger.

TRY A SECTION HIKE
Head north or south along the white-blazed trail. North leads to the South River Picnic Area and overlooks; south takes you toward Loft Mountain. Choose your distance—either direction offers a half-day escape with scenic payoffs.

TIPS

- Campsites at Loft Mountain are first come, first serve
- Start early—parking fills by 10 a.m. on weekends
- This stretch can be buggy—pack repellent
- Watch for bears and store food properly

THINGS TO DO

BRING THE KIDS
For a lighter outing, the AT crosses Skyline Drive just minutes from Swift Run Gap. Park nearby and take a short out-and-back hike to sample the trail without committing to a full trek.

CAMP AT LOFT MOUNTAIN
About 20 minutes south of Swift Run Gap, Loft Mountain Campground sits right on the AT. Book a site for the weekend, enjoy the camp store and amphitheater, and watch the stars emerge from your picnic table.

SPOT WILDLIFE & WILDFLOWERS
Deer and black bears roam this part of the park, but sightings are usually at a distance. Spring brings redbud and trillium, while summer offers mountain laurel and flame azalea. Bring binoculars and a field guide.

TIPS

- Wear layers—the ridge gets windy fast
- Stop at Loft Mountain Wayside for maps & snacks
- Bring $30 for Shenandoah's park entrance fee
- Keep kids and dogs close near drop-offs

APPALACHIAN TRAIL

BUDGET TRAVEL

WHERE TO STAY

Loft Mountain Campground sits right on the Appalachian Trail and offers wooded sites, mountain views, and access to a camp store for basic supplies. If you'd rather sleep indoors, nearby towns like Ruckersville, Elkton, and Gordonsville have affordable motels and simple Airbnbs—many under $100 a night and just a short drive from the trail.

WHAT TO EAT

Fuel up without breaking the bank at a few local favorites. In Gordonsville, Patch Brewing Co. serves up hearty burgers and craft beer in a laid-back setting. Harrisonburg's Grilled Cheese Mania is beloved for its creative takes on a comfort classic, while Elkton's Grub & Grab offers quick, satisfying meals perfect after a long day on the trail.

SAMPLE ITINERARY

• Friday: Arrive and settle into an Airbnb in Elkton or a tent site at Loft Mountain.

• Saturday: Hike to Hightop, picnic at South River Falls, grab a dinner at Patch in Gordonsville.

• Sunday: Take a sunrise walk, stop for coffee in Ruckersville, and enjoy a scenic drive home.

LUXURY TRAVEL

WHERE TO STAY

Barboursville's 1804 Inn offers vineyard charm, while Lydia Mountain Lodge features private cabins with mountain views. Friendly City Inn in Harrisonburg blends boutique comfort with walkable access to shops and cafés. For a more secluded option, try a private cottage in Gordonsville.

WHAT TO EAT

Enjoy fine Italian cuisine and wine pairings at Palladio Restaurant at Barboursville Vineyards. For a refined meal within driving distance of the trail, try seasonal Southern fare at Well Hung in Gordonsville or a multi-course dinner at the Joshua Wilton House in Harrisonburg.

SAMPLE ITINERARY

- Friday: Arrive at a vineyard inn and enjoy a chef's tasting with wine pairings.

- Saturday: Hike a scenic stretch of the AT, then relax with a massage or soaking tub.

- Sunday: Brunch in Gordonsville and a slow country drive home.

UNDER 2 HOURS

QUICK TRIPS

VIRGINIA BEACH

DISTANCE FROM RVA
1 hour 45 minutes by car

GEOGRAPHY
SE Virginia, where the Atlantic Ocean meets the Chesapeake Bay

BEST TIME TO VISIT
Late spring through early fall for beach weather

GENERAL VIBE
Fun-loving, lively, and summery—great for families, couples, water-sports enthusiasts, and nostalgic beach seekers.

WHY ITS WORTH THE TRIP

Virginia Beach is where laid-back beach town energy meets family-friendly fun and vibrant coastal culture. With wide sandy shores, a classic boardwalk, and endless seafood spots, it's the kind of place where you can unplug—or pack your itinerary. Whether you're after surf and sand, dolphin cruises, or late-night arcade nostalgia, it's all just a short drive away.

EXPLORE MORE

SANDBRIDGE, VA | 25 MIN. S

This quiet beach enclave offers fewer crowds, wide stretches of sand, and access to Back Bay National Wildlife Refuge. It's a serene alternative to the bustling Oceanfront District and a favorite spot for local surfers.

PUNGO, VA | 15 MIN. SW

A rural community with pick-your-own farms, produce stands, and the Military Aviation Museum- a gem featuring vintage aircraft and seasonal airshows. Don't miss The Bee & The Biscuit, a popular spot for farm-to-table brunch.

CHESAPEAKE, VA | 25 MIN. W

Head inland for paddle trails, nature parks, and the Great Dismal Swamp National Wildlife Refuge—ideal for birdwatching, flatwater kayaking, and spotting wildlife. Chesapeake offers a quieter, greener side of the region.

About 1 hour 45 minutes by car via I-64 E, Virginia Beach is best accessed by driving. Traffic can be heavy in summer, so consider leaving early. Parking near the beach can be tight—look for hotel lots or public decks off the boardwalk.

TIPS

VIRGINIA BEACH

THINGS TO DO

FIRST LANDING STATE PARK
Explore 20+ miles of hiking/biking trails through maritime forest, swamps, and sand dunes at this historic state park—the site where English colonists first landed in 1607. It's a peaceful, nature-rich escape just minutes from the beach.

EXPLORE THE BEACHES
From the lively 3-mile boardwalk at the Oceanfront to the peaceful stretches of Sandbridge and Chesapeake Bay, Virginia Beach has a shoreline for you. Local spots like Croatan and Chic's Beach offer laid-back charm and easygoing fun.

WATERSPORTS, BOAT OR KAYAK TOURS
Whether you're after high-speed thrills or tranquil exploration, there's something on the water for you. Take a dolphin-watching cruise, charter a fishing boat, or paddle your way through coastal waterways and inlets by kayak.

TIPS

- Visit in September for fewer crowds and warm water
- Browse local art at ViBe Creative District
- Climb Cape Henry Lighthouse for panoramic views
- Grab handmade taffy and fudge at Forbes Candies

THINGS TO DO

SURFING LESSONS
Virginia Beach is a great place to catch your first wave. Local surf schools offer beginner-friendly lessons and equipment rentals, while calm backwaters are ideal for stand-up paddleboarding. Plan ahead, these tours are tide dependent.

MOTOR WORLD
A local favorite, Motor World features go-karts, bumper boats, mini golf, and paintball. With multiple tracks and challenges, it's a fun, fast-paced, high-energy alternative to the usual beach scene, especially for thrill seekers.

OCEAN BREEZE WATERPARK
This family-friendly waterpark has a tropical island theme and over 30 rides and attractions, from lazy rivers to high-speed slides. It's a great way to beat the heat and mix up your beach getaway with some splashy, sun-soaked fun.

TIPS

- Rent a beach cruiser and enjoy a boardwalk ride
- Go ghost crabbing by flashlight on the beach at night
- Spot swamp rainbows amid the cypress at First Landing
- Pose with the animal statues at Jungle Golf

VIRGINIA BEACH

BUDGET TRAVEL

WHERE TO STAY

Affordable beachfront stays are within reach in Virginia Beach. Look for budget-friendly Airbnbs in the Oceanfront or Chesapeake Beach areas. Hotels like Surfbreak and Oceans 2700 often offer rates under $100 per night. For slightly higher budgets, The Atrium, Red Roof PLUS+ and Sandcastle Resort typically stay under $130 per night.

WHAT TO EAT

Grab pizza by the slice at Chicho's Pizza Express, enjoy casual tacos and drinks at Baja Cantina, sip local brews at Vibrant Shore Brewing Company, dig into seafood baskets at Waterman's Surfside Grill, and cool off with homemade scoops from Lolly's Creamery, a boardwalk favorite.

SAMPLE ITINERARY

• Friday: Check in and stroll the boardwalk for casual eats and beach views. Rent a bike and ride to the ViBe District or the quiet north end.

• Saturday: Beach day, then visit the aquarium or a local park. Try ghost crabbing after dark.

• Sunday: Sunrise walk and one last oceanfront coffee before heading home.

LUXURY TRAVEL

WHERE TO STAY

Book a room at the historic Cavalier Hotel, The Founders Inn and Spa, or a modern oceanfront suite like the Hilton Vacation Club. For a more private stay, consider a high-end beachfront condo on Airbnb. Many luxury properties offer on-site dining, full-service spas, or easy beach access—perfect for a relaxed, upscale weekend.

WHAT TO EAT

Dine at Orion's Roof for Asian-fusion and views, Becca for elegant garden-to-table fare, or Ruth's Chris for classic steaks. Heirloom serves creative farm-to-table dishes, Steinhilber's offers seafood in a historic setting, and Terrapin features contemporary American cuisine. For cocktails with a view, visit The Hunt Room.

SAMPLE ITINERARY

- Friday: Arrive in time for sunset cocktails and a waterfront dinner.

- Saturday: Start with a morning charter boat trip, then unwind with a spa treatment and enjoy a gourmet dinner.

- Sunday: Savor a champagne brunch, visit the aquarium, and grab a fresh seafood lunch.

QUICK TRIPS

FIRST LANDING

DISTANCE FROM RVA
2 hours by car

GEOGRAPHY
Coastal Virginia, at the edge of the Chesapeake Bay in Virginia Beach

BEST TIME TO VISIT
Spring and fall for trails; summer for beach days.

GENERAL VIBE
Peaceful, wooded, and coastal—great for campers, paddlers, and anyone who wants a quiet escape.

WHY ITS WORTH THE TRIP

Tucked between the Chesapeake Bay and the bustle of Virginia Beach, First Landing State Park is a coastal escape that feels both wild and peaceful. The site of the 1607 English landing, it's rich in history—but it's the windswept swamps, golden trails, and quiet paths that draw weekend wanderers. Paddle mossy inlets, walk beneath towering pines, or stretch out on a peaceful beach.

EXPLORE MORE

CAPE HENRY & FORT STORY | 10 MIN. E

Visit the historic Cape Henry Lighthouse and the site of the settlers' first landing in 1607. The views are stunning, and you can climb the original 1792 lighthouse on select days for a unique look at the coast.

VIBE CREATIVE DISTRICT | 15 MIN. S

A local arts and culture hub in Virginia Beach with murals, cafés, vintage shops, and handmade goods. Great for a low-key afternoon and supporting local artists.

CHESAPEAKE BAY BEACHES | 10 MIN. N

Quieter than the oceanfront, these bay-side beaches are ideal for swimming, reading, or a peaceful walk along the shore. Shallow waters and gentle waves make them especially great for families or low-key beach goers.

TIPS

Easily accessed by car via I-64 E to Route 60. Once inside the park, roads are well marked. Parking can fill up fast in summer, so arrive early. The park is close enough to pair with other Virginia Beach attractions, but also self-contained enough for a complete weekend.

FIRST LANDING

THINGS TO DO

VISIT THE TRAIL CENTER

Stop by the First Landing Trail Center for maps, local insight, and educational exhibits about the park's unique ecosystems and history. It's a great place to start your visit or get oriented before hitting the trails.

HIKE OR BIKE THE TRAILS

Explore over 20 miles of trails through maritime forest, freshwater swamps, and dunes. The Bald Cypress Trail is a favorite for its otherworldly swamp views and hanging moss.

RELAX ON THE BEACH

The park's private Bay-side beach is great for swimming, sunbathing, and picnics—with gentler waves than the oceanfront. No lifeguards, so swim at your own risk.

TIPS

- Reserve campsites and cabins early in spring and fall
- Wear water shoes for paddling or swampy trails
- Pack bug spray—mosquitoes and ticks are common
- Arrive early on summer weekends—parking fills up fast

THINGS TO DO

PADDLE THE WATERWAYS

Launch a kayak or paddleboard into Broad Bay or Long Creek for a serene trip through protected coves, often accompanied by egrets, herons, and osprey overhead.

SPOT WILDLIFE

Turtles, crabs, birds, and the occasional fox make this a surprisingly biodiverse coastal zone. Visit early morning or dusk for the best sightings.

CAMP OR STAY IN A CABIN

Whether you're pitching a tent, pulling in an RV, or staying in one of the rustic cabins, First Landing offers overnight options just steps from the trails and shoreline.

TIPS

- Alcohol isn't allowed on the beach
- Learn park rules & safety guidelines before you arrive
- Store food securely—wildlife may visit campsites
- Catch a spectacular sunrise or sunset from the beach

FIRST LANDING

BUDGET TRAVEL

WHERE TO STAY
Tent and RV camping is available within the park, as well as rustic cabins with full kitchens. Outside the park, look for motels or Airbnbs near Shore Drive for affordable, close-to-nature stays.

WHAT TO EAT
Pack a cooler with essentials, or head just outside the park for casual eats like Simple Eats or Leaping Lizard Café. For a treat, grab handmade fudge or saltwater taffy from the nearby Forbes Candies.

SAMPLE ITINERARY

• Friday: Arrive and stroll the Bald Cypress Trail before a sunset picnic on the beach.

• Saturday: Paddle the waterways or bike the Cape Henry Trail, then explore the ViBe District and return for a campfire dinner.

• Sunday: Watch the sunrise, grab coffee nearby, and enjoy one last beach walk.

LUXURY TRAVEL

WHERE TO STAY

While the park itself is rustic, nearby hotels and vacation rentals on Shore Drive or in Chesapeake Beach (Chic's Beach) offer upscale options with water views. Look for beachfront condos or boutique inns with easy access to the park.

WHAT TO EAT

For a splurge, dine at Eurasia Café (seasonal fine dining with coastal flair) or Tautog's for upscale seafood in a historic cottage setting. Pair your beach weekend with fresh oysters and chilled white wine.

SAMPLE ITINERARY

• Friday: Check into a bayfront suite and enjoy cocktails with a view.

• Saturday: Hike and paddle in the park, then spend the afternoon exploring local shops and dining al fresco.

• Sunday: Brunch by the water and a quiet walk through the cypress before heading home.

QUICK TRIPS

WASHINGTON, D.C.

DISTANCE FROM RVA

2 hours by car or train

GEOGRAPHY

Mid-Atlantic, at the confluence of the Potomac and Anacostia Rivers

BEST TIME TO VISIT

Spring for blossoms, fall for fewer crowds

GENERAL VIBE

Dynamic, cultured, and full of contrasts—ideal for curious travelers, museum lovers, history buffs, and city explorers.

WHY ITS WORTH THE TRIP

Washington, DC is more than politics and monuments—though those are certainly here in abundance. It's a city of layered stories, world-class museums (most free), and neighborhoods with everything from indie coffeehouses and rooftop bars to historic row houses and global cuisine. Walking the National Mall or browsing an arts market, DC offers something surprising around every corner.

EXPLORE MORE

ALEXANDRIA, VA | 20 MIN. S

A charming historic town on the Potomac River with cobblestone streets, waterfront dining, and boutique shopping. Walk the Old Town, take a ghost tour, or hop on a water taxi.

SILVER SPRING, MD | 20 MIN. N

A lively, walkable suburb with global eats, indie theaters, public art, and easy Metro access. It's home to some of the best Ethiopian food in the country and makes a great side trip for lunch, a show, or a stroll through downtown.

GREAT FALLS PARK, VA | 30 MIN. W

An awe-inspiring natural area with dramatic waterfalls and hiking trails along the Potomac Gorge. Perfect for a breath of fresh air just outside the city, and popular with hikers, climbers, and photographers.

TIPS

DC is easily reached from Richmond via Amtrak's Northeast Regional or by car along I-95. Traffic can be heavy, so allow extra time around the Beltway. Once in the city, skip driving and use the Metro, buses, rideshares, or bike and scooter shares. Most major sights are walkable within the National Mall area.

WASHINGTON, D.C.

THINGS TO DO

THE SMITHSONIAN MUSEUMS

Spend an afternoon—or a whole weekend—exploring any of the free museums on the National Mall. Favorites include the National Museum of African American History and Culture, the Air and Space Museum, and the National Gallery of Art.

MONUMENTS BY MOONLIGHT

See the Lincoln, Jefferson, and Martin Luther King, Jr. memorials in a new light with an evening stroll or guided tour. Glowing lights and quieter paths give the monuments a more reflective feel—a peaceful way to experience the National Mall.

UNION MARKET & LA COSECHA

Side-by-side warehouse markets with global eats, craft cocktails, and local goods. Grab lunch from a top vendor and explore Latin American makers at La Cosecha—just a short walk from the NoMa Metro.

TIPS

- See cherry blossoms at the Tidal Basin in early spring
- Bike the National Mall for easy, scenic sightseeing
- Visit the Library of Congress for the architecture
- Tour the Capitol or White House (book ahead)

THINGS TO DO

LUNCH IN ADAMS MORGAN

Known for its global flavors and colorful street scene, Adams Morgan is a great spot to grab lunch—whether it's empanadas, Ethiopian, or falafel—and take in one of DC's most diverse and lively neighborhoods.

VISIT GEORGETOWN

From riverside walks to cobblestone streets, Georgetown blends history, shopping, and scenic charm. Browse boutiques and bakeries, explore the C&O Canal, grab a drink by the water, or rent a kayak for a different view of the city.

BLAGDEN ALLEY

Tucked behind row houses in Shaw, Blagden Alley is a hidden pocket full of bold murals, craft cocktails, and creative energy. Wander the cobbled alleyways to find speakeasies, indie coffee shops & street art, all packed into a few atmospheric blocks.

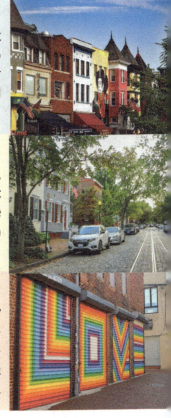

TIPS

- Explore the Folger Shakespeare Library
- Marvel at the National Bonsai & Penjing Museum
- Visit the O Street Mansion or Barbie Pond for quirky fun
- Wander Hirshhorn Sculpture Garden (reopens 2026)

WASHINGTON, D.C.

BUDGET TRAVEL

WHERE TO STAY

Look for boutique hotels or stylish hostels in neighborhoods like NoMa, Capitol Hill, or Dupont Circle—areas that balance character with convenience. The Moxy DC, Generator Hostel, or Sonder units often have weekend deals. Proximity to Metro is key for savings and ease.

WHAT TO EAT

For tasty budget bites in DC, head to Super Tacos in Adams Morgan or La Tejana in Mount Pleasant. Grab a bagel sandwich at Call Your Mother, or hit Eggholic for Indian-inspired breakfast. Pho Viet offers comforting bowls on the cheap, while Busboys and Poets blends books and bites. Don't miss a cupcake from Baked & Wired.

SAMPLE ITINERARY

- Friday: Arrive by train, stroll the National Mall before dinner in Chinatown

- Saturday: Tour the monuments, visit museums, explore Union Market and La Cosecha.

- Sunday: Brunch in Shaw or Adams Morgan, one last museum, then catch an afternoon train home.

LUXURY TRAVEL

WHERE TO STAY

For a luxurious stay, choose from The Line Hotel in Adams Morgan, the historic Hay-Adams near the White House, or the sleek Conrad DC with rooftop views. For extra indulgence, consider the Rosewood Washington DC or the stylish Dupont Circle Hotel, both offering high-end comfort in walkable, central neighborhoods.

WHAT TO EAT

Book a table at Bourbon Steak for prime cuts and elegance, or indulge in a tasting menu at José Andrés' acclaimed minibar. The Dabney and Le Diplomate offer refined takes on regional and French cuisine, while Café Milano remains a Georgetown classic. For cocktails, try barmini, Off the Record, or the historic Round Robin Bar.

SAMPLE ITINERARY

• Friday: Check in, cocktails with a view, dine at a top chef's table.

• Saturday: Book a museum tour or gallery hop, visit a spa, then enjoy dinner and a show.

• Sunday: Savor a late brunch, browse boutiques in Georgetown, and make your way home relaxed.

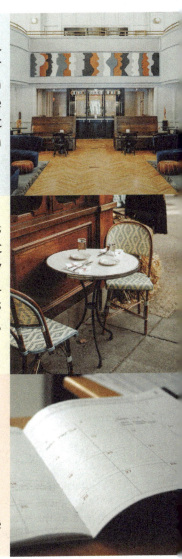

QUICK TRIPS
MIDDLEBURG

DISTANCE FROM RVA

2 hr 10 min by car

GEOGRAPHY

Northern Virginia, in Loudoun County's horse and wine country

BEST TIME TO VISIT

Spring blooms, fall foliage, vineyard season

GENERAL VIBE

Upscale, scenic, and charming—ideal for couples, wine lovers, and those craving a sophisticated countryside escape

WHY ITS WORTH THE TRIP

Middleburg is pure Virginia elegance with rolling countryside, wine tastings, antique shops, and winding roads flanked by stone fences. But beneath its polished surface is a welcoming, quietly creative town with deep history and an outdoorsy side. From a vineyard picnic to a day hike on the nearby Appalachian Trail, Middleburg delivers a perfect blend of refined and rustic.

EXPLORE MORE

FRONT ROYAL, VA | 35 MIN. W

Known as the "Gateway to Skyline Drive," Front Royal pairs small-town charm with big outdoor access. Explore Main Street or head into Shenandoah National Park. Local outfitters rent canoes and kayaks for river trips.

BLUEMONT, VA | 30 MIN. W

Access the Appalachian Trail at Bear's Den Trail Center for a short but rewarding hike to stunning overlooks. It's one of the most scenic day hikes in Northern Virginia. Afterward, unwind with wine and valley views at nearby Bluemont Vineyard.

LEESBURG, VA | 25 MIN. NE

For a livelier outing, head to Leesburg for cobblestone streets lined with cafés, antique shops, and local boutiques. If you're in the mood to splurge, the Leesburg Premium Outlets offer major brand deals just minutes from downtown.

TIPS

Reach Middleburg via I-95 N and Route 50 W. The town is small and walkable, but you'll need a car to explore nearby vineyards and trailheads. Parking is free and usually easy to find, though weekends can be busy.

MIDDLEBURG

THINGS TO DO

WINE TASTING & VINEYARDS

Loudoun County is home to more than 40 wineries, many with scenic patios and sweeping views. For a classic Middleburg experience, start with tastings at Greenhill Vineyards or Cana Vineyards, both just minutes from downtown.

NATIONAL SPORTING LIBRARY & MUSEUM

This museum highlights the region's equestrian and sporting heritage through rotating exhibits, rare books, and fine art. It's a quiet, elegant place to spend an hour or two, especially on a rainy day.

BOUTIQUES & GALLERIES

Washington Street is lined with upscale boutiques, indie bookshops, and local galleries. Shop for antiques, equestrian gifts, and fine art—or just take a leisurely stroll and window browse between cafés.

TIPS

- Book tastings early—weekends fill fast
- Smart casual beats hiking boots when indoors here
- Check for music or art on the green
- April and October bring peak color

THINGS TO DO

STEEPLECHASE OR POLO MATCH
Middleburg's spring races and summer polo matches are long-standing local traditions. Bring a picnic and dress the part—spectating here means champagne flutes, wide-brimmed hats, and a genteel countryside vibe.

MT. DEFIANCE CIDERY & DISTILLERY
Located just off Main Street, Mt. Defiance offers small-batch ciders and spirits in a relaxed setting. Sample their handcrafted beverages in the tasting room or enjoy a drink on the patio, making it a fun stop for those looking to explore.

SCENIC DRIVES & COUNTRY ROADS
Surrounding Middleburg are some of Virginia's prettiest back roads. Drive Snickersville Turnpike or Route 50 to see rolling hills, white-fenced farms, and stone bridges—an ideal way to take in horse country at its finest.

TIPS

- Balance wine with a short Bluemont hike
- Jackie O signed the Red Fox guest book
- Don't pet the polo ponies—they're working
- Even the gas station stocks good wine here

MIDDLEBURG

BUDGET TRAVEL

WHERE TO STAY

Budget stays in Middleburg are limited, but the Best Western in Leesburg is a reliable choice. For something more private, consider Airbnbs like the Cottage at Stonecroft or a carriage house rental in nearby Round Hill.

WHAT TO EAT

For casual eats, try Common Grounds for coffee and breakfast, Teddy's for pizza and subs, or Scruffy's for ice cream. Red Bar Sushi is a local favorite, and the seasonal Middleburg Community Farmers Market is great for picnic supplies.

SAMPLE ITINERARY

• Friday: Arrive and stroll downtown, then dine casually at a local pub.

• Saturday: Visit vineyards in the morning, hike to Bear's Den in the afternoon, and enjoy dinner at a bistro or wine bar.

• Sunday: Brunch and antique browsing before the drive home.

LUXURY TRAVEL

WHERE TO STAY

Book a stay at the Salamander Resort & Spa for full-service luxury in the heart of Middleburg, with spa treatments, riding lessons, fine dining, and easy access to trails and vineyards. For a quieter alternative, consider The Ashby Inn, a romantic country retreat just a short drive away.

WHAT TO EAT

Dine at the Harrimans Virginia Piedmont Grill for refined seasonal cuisine or enjoy an upscale meal at Red Fox Inn & Tavern, one of the oldest inns in America with candlelit charm and Southern hospitality.

SAMPLE ITINERARY

• Friday: Arrive, check in, and enjoy cocktails at the resort.

• Saturday: Spa treatments, vineyard tours, and an afternoon hike with sunset views.

• Sunday: Sleep in, then enjoy a gourmet brunch before the scenic drive back.

QUICK TRIPS

LURAY

DISTANCE FROM RVA

2 hrs 30 min by car

GEOGRAPHY

NW Virginia, Shenandoah Valley, near the Blue Ridge Mountains

BEST TIME TO VISIT

Spring blooms, fall colors, year-round caverns

GENERAL VIBE

Earthy, peaceful, and naturally beautiful—ideal for hikers, families, and travelers in need of a quiet recharge.

WHY ITS WORTH THE TRIP

Luray is a small town known for its impressive natural landscape. While Luray Caverns draws many visitors with its vast underground formations, the area also offers easy access to Skyline Drive, Shenandoah National Park, and the scenic Hawksbill Greenway—making it ideal for hiking, biking, and quiet outdoor escapes.

EXPLORE MORE

STANLEY, VA | 10 MIN. S

This tiny town offers peaceful farmland views and easy access to local hiking trails. Don't miss a stop at Hawksbill Diner for a classic country breakfast. Stanley also makes a great base for exploring Shenandoah National Park without the crowds.

RILEYVILLE, VA | 15 MIN. N

A quiet community along the Shenandoah River, perfect for kayaking, tubing, or scenic riverbank picnics. It's a peaceful place to unplug, with wooded cabins and sweeping mountain views just minutes from Luray.

SHENANDOAH, VA | 25 MIN. SE

A small railroad town with river access and mountain views. Great for a slower-paced drive or walking tour. Shenandoah also offers a glimpse into the region's industrial past, with historic buildings and a relaxed, hometown feel.

About 2 hours and 30 minutes from Richmond by car via US-33 and US-211, Luray is best reached by driving. While public transit options are limited, parking is easy and the scenic route through the Blue Ridge adds to the experience.

TIPS

LURAY

THINGS TO DO

STONY MAN MOUNTAIN HIKE

Located just inside Shenandoah National Park, this short but stunning trail offers some of the best panoramic views in the region. It's a great option for all skill levels, with a peaceful summit perfect for sunrise or a picnic.

LURAY CAVERNS

The largest caverns in the eastern U.S., this sub-terranean wonderland features towering stone columns, mirrored pools, and the hauntingly beautiful sounds of the Great Stalacpipe Organ. It's a surreal experience worth checking out.

HAWKSBILL GREENWAY

This paved trail runs alongside Hawksbill Creek and through the heart of downtown Luray. It's ideal for a gentle walk, jog, or bike ride, with benches, birdwatching spots, and public art scattered along the way.

TIPS

- The Luray Singing Tower rings out on warm months
- For a quieter Shenandoah hike enter at Thornton Gap
- Book Caverns tickets in advance during peak seasons
- Cooter's hosts free weekend bluegrass shows

THINGS TO DO

SHENANDOAH HERITAGE VILLAGE
Part of the Luray Caverns complex, this open-air museum features 19th-century buildings arranged like a small historic village. Often overlooked for the Caverns, it's a charming, photo-worthy destination with real historical value.

BIRDSONG PLEASURE GARDEN
A peaceful, privately owned garden open by appointment, Birdsong features beautifully landscaped paths, mountain views, and a wide variety of plants. It's a quiet, off-the-radar retreat for garden lovers and anyone seeking a slower pace.

CAR AND CARRIAGE CARAVAN MUSEUM
Located near the Luray Caverns entrance, this small museum showcases antique vehicles from the 18th to 20th centuries—including carriages, wagons, and early motorcars. It's a solid stop for anyone interested in transportation history.

TIPS

- Grab pie or peanut soup at the historic Mimslyn Inn
- The Hawksbill Greenway is lit for evening strolls
- Gathering Grounds serves great coffee and sandwiches
- Arts & Artisans showcases work by local artists

LURAY

BUDGET TRAVEL

WHERE TO STAY

For an affordable stay with local character, Hillside Motel offers retro charm, mountain views, and seasonal pool access just outside town—often under $100 a night. For something a little nicer that still fits a modest budget, standard rooms at The Mimslyn Inn occasionally dip near $120 and come with historic charm and on-site dining.

WHAT TO EAT

Grab a sandwich or salad at West Main Market. Gathering Grounds serves up house-made pies, baked goods, and strong coffee in a cozy café atmosphere. For dinner, try Asian Station for Thai and Japanese dishes, or head to Triple Crown BBQ for smoked meats and homemade sides just off the highway.

SAMPLE ITINERARY

• Friday: Check in, and then take a walk on the Hawksbill Greenway. Dinner at Asian Station.

• Saturday: Tour Luray Caverns, the village, and labyrinth; dinner at Triple Crown BBQ and a pint at Hawksbill Brewing.

• Sunday: Morning hike in Shenandoah, coffee at Gathering Grounds, then a scenic drive home.

LUXURY TRAVEL

WHERE TO STAY

For a luxurious escape, Luray Mountain Cabins offers scenic views and private hot tubs. In town, consider Piney Hill Bed & Breakfast, Hotel Laurance, Inn of the Shenandoah, South Court Inn, or Mayneview B&B—each known for comfort, character, and warm hospitality.

WHAT TO EAT

For a refined meal, try Circa '31 at the Mimslyn Inn, known for its elegant setting and seasonal menus. The Speakeasy Bar & Restaurant offers classic cocktails and hearty entrees in a vintage setting, while The Chop House Bistro delivers steaks, seafood, and an intimate, upscale dining experience.

SAMPLE ITINERARY

- Friday: Check in and watch the sunset, then dine at The Chop House Bistro.

- Saturday: Tour the Caverns, book a spa visit, and enjoy dinner and drinks at The Speakeasy.

- Sunday: Have breakfast in town, tour Birdsong Pleasure Garden, then cruise Skyline Drive home.

QUICK TRIPS

CLIFTON FORGE

DISTANCE FROM RVA

2 hrs 30 min by car

GEOGRAPHY

Alleghany Highlands, along the Jackson River in western Virginia

BEST TIME TO VISIT

Fall foliage, spring blooms, summer fun

GENERAL VIBE

Creative, nostalgic, and community-driven—perfect for artists, train lovers, couples, and laid-back explorers.

WHY ITS WORTH THE TRIP

Clifton Forge is one of those small towns where the past hasn't vanished—it's settled in comfortably. For such a quiet place, it's incredibly active, with galleries, live music, and community events around every corner. Walk the historic streets, hike riverside trails, or ride the scenic railway. With nearby Douthat State Park, Clifton Forge offers a cozy, culture-meets-nature weekend that feels like stepping into a storybook.

EXPLORE MORE

DOUTHAT STATE PARK, VA | 15 MIN. E

A gem for hiking, biking, paddling, and vibrant fall color. Swim or fish in the lake, explore wooded trails, or stay overnight in a 1930s cabin. The park also offers scenic overlooks, picnic spots, and quiet moments just beyond the town's edge.

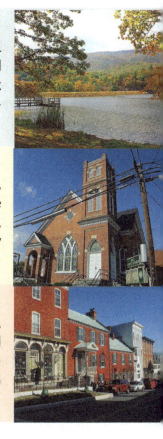

COVINGTON, VA | 20 MIN. W

Larger and more industrial than Clifton Forge, Covington still offers small-town charm. Explore its historic district, walk the Jackson River Trail, or visit Humpback Bridge—the oldest and only curved covered bridge in Virginia.

LEXINGTON, VA | 30 MIN. SE

A college town full of history, walkable streets, and creative flair. Tour VMI, browse galleries and museums, or go treasure hunting at Duke's Antiques. Just Games offers a dose of nostalgia with board games, retro finds, and local energy.

Best reached by car via I-64 West. Downtown Clifton Forge is walkable, but you'll want a car to explore nearby parks, landmarks, and scenic byways. Amtrak's Cardinal line stops here three days a week, with service available from Richmond via transfer in Alexandria.

TIPS

75

CLIFTON FORGE

THINGS TO DO

C&O RAILWAY HERITAGE CENTER
A must-see for train lovers and history buffs. Explore restored locomotives, vintage rail cars, and an interactive museum that tells the story of Clifton Forge's railroading legacy. The grounds also host seasonal events and special exhibits.

MASONIC THEATER & AMPHITHEATRE
Catch a show at the Masonic Theatre or its award-winning outdoor amphitheater, then stroll Ridgeway Street to browse quirky shops, working galleries, and local cafés. The district blends small-town warmth with a lively creative spirit.

CLIFTON FORGE SCHOOL OF THE ARTS
A creative hub offering classes, exhibits, and handmade goods in historic downtown buildings. Browse local artwork, attend a workshop, or simply enjoy the vibrant atmosphere that supports artists of all ages and skill levels.

TIPS

- Grab a local brew and a bite at Jack Mason's Tavern
- Locals call the mural-covered building "5-Sides"
- Enjoy vintage-style ice cream at C & Oh! Ice Cream Depot
- Check for festivals and music nights year-round

THINGS TO DO

HUMPBACK BRIDGE
Just outside Covington, this is Virginia's oldest surviving covered bridge—and the only one with a curved design. Picnic tables, a grassy field, and seasonal art make it a charming roadside stop.

SMITH CREEK SENSORY TRAIL
This short, inclusive trail is designed to engage every sense. With textured paths, sounds of nature, and interactive features, it's perfect for families, accessible outings, or anyone seeking a peaceful walk.

NATURAL BRIDGE STATE PARK
A short drive brings you to this dramatic natural wonder. Walk beneath the soaring limestone arch, hike along Cedar Creek, explore the Monacan Indian Village, or join a ranger-led nature talk.

TIPS

- Visit in October for peak foliage and crisp mountain air
- Pick up olive oil at OLuv Oil or sweets at Sweetest Side
- Bring hiking shoes—Douthat's trails are worth the detour
- Shop regional art at Alleghany Highlands Arts & Crafts

CLIFTON FORGE

BUDGET TRAVEL

WHERE TO STAY

The Red Lantern Inn offers a cozy stay in the heart of downtown, steps from shops and galleries. For a peaceful retreat, book a renovated 1930s cabin at Douthat State Park—surprisingly stylish inside and close to trails and the lake. Affordable Airbnbs under $125 a night are also available in and around town.

WHAT TO EAT

Jack Mason's Tavern is the town favorite for hearty pub fare, house brews, and live music on the weekends. For a casual lunch, try 42 Deli or Mountain Field Market, both offering sandwiches and snacks with a local touch. Sweeten the day with a scoop at C & Oh! Ice Cream Depot, or head over to Covington for fresh coffee at Manic Coffee.

SAMPLE ITINERARY

- Friday: Arrive, stroll downtown, dine at Family TreeT's, and grab ice cream at C & Oh!

- Saturday: Visit the rail museum, browse galleries, then walk the Sensory Trail or hike at Douthat. Dinner and a pint at Jack Mason's.

- Sunday: Coffee at Manic and antique browsing in Covington before heading home.

LUXURY TRAVEL

WHERE TO STAY

Ridgely Bed, Breakfast, and Historic Gardens offers polished comfort, curated interiors, and garden views just minutes from town center. Hillcrest Mansion Inn is another elegant option, with stately architecture, spacious rooms, and mountain views from the wraparound porch. Both inns provide a quiet, high-end retreat perfect for anyone seeking refined comfort.

WHAT TO EAT

Start with a relaxed breakfast at Family TreeT's Café, and plan dinner at The Cat and Owl in Covington. For something casual, try BBQ at Roller's or wood-fired pies at Cucci's Pizzeria. End the night with cocktails and live jazz at Haywood's Piano Bar in Lexington—but note that most local spots close early. Pick up a bottle to enjoy back at your B&B.

SAMPLE ITINERARY

• Friday: Settle in, then enjoy cocktails and dinner at The Cat and Owl.

• Saturday: Hike Douthat, picnic by the lake, browse the shops and galleries in town. Grab a delicious ice cream at C & Oh!

• Sunday: Brunch at Family TreeT's, antique browsing in Covington, and a scenic drive home.

QUICK TRIPS

DOUTHAT

DISTANCE FROM RVA

2 hrs 30 min by car

GEOGRAPHY

Appalachian foothills in western Virginia's Alleghany Highlands

BEST TIME TO VISIT

Spring wildflowers, summer lake days, fall hikes

GENERAL VIBE

Tranquil, outdoorsy, and rustic—perfect for families, hikers, and those seeking to unplug.

WHY ITS WORTH THE TRIP

One of Virginia's original state parks, Douthat is a quiet mountain escape with over 40 miles of trails, a 50-acre lake for swimming and fishing, and hand-built cabins dating to the 1930s. Visitors can paddle or boat across calm waters, picnic along forested shorelines, and watch for deer and songbirds amid the hardwood forests. A perfect blend of history, nature, and solitude.

EXPLORE MORE

CLIFTON FORGE, VA | 15 MIN. SW

A historic railroad town with a thriving arts scene. Visit the C&O Railway Heritage Center, explore downtown, or catch a performance at the open-air Masonic Amphitheatre. Antique shops and friendly vibes round out the experience.

HOT SPRINGS, VA | 40 MIN. S

This elegant mountain town is best known for the Omni Homestead Resort, a historic landmark with warm mineral springs and golf courses. Stroll the village streets, book a spa treatment, or explore nearby hiking trails and scenic drives.

FINCASTLE, VA | 40 MIN. SE

Founded in 1772, this historic town features over 50 preserved buildings, a local history museum, and tree-lined streets ideal for a self-guided walking tour. Antique shops and galleries add to its small-town charm.

TIPS

Douthat is about 2.5 hours from Richmond via I-64 W, with direct access from Exit 27 to Douthat State Park Road. The drive is scenic and easy to follow as you approach the Alleghany Highlands. There's no public transportation to the park, so driving is essential. Cell service can be limited, so be sure to download maps and check your route in advance.

DOUTHAT

THINGS TO DO

TOBACCO HOUSE RIDGE TRAIL

This moderate 2.3-mile out-and-back trail rewards hikers with lake views and a cascading waterfall created by the dam. It starts near White Oak Campground and climbs to a bench-lined overlook.

HIKE OR BIKE THE TRAILS

Douthat is a favorite for mountain bikers, with 24 of its 26 trails open to bikes. More than 40 miles of routes wind through the Allegheny Mountains, from easy loops to steep climbs for both riders and hikers.

FISH DOUTHAT LAKE AND WILSON CREEK

Fish the 50-acre Douthat Lake, stocked seasonally with rainbow, brown, and brook trout. You'll also find bass, crappie, pickerel, and catfish. A youth-only trout area is located on Wilson Creek below the dam.

TIPS

- Hit the beach early or near sunset
- Daily entrance & parking is $7
- Fishing requires a valid permit or license
- Store food securely to avoid wildlife issues

THINGS TO DO

WATER ACTIVITIES ON THE LAKE
From Memorial Day through Labor Day, visitors can rent canoes, kayaks, paddleboats, and Jon boats with trolling motors. Swimming is allowed in the designated beach area during the same season—a great way to cool off.

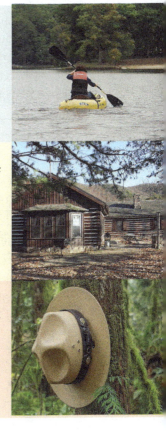

STAY IN A HISTORIC 1930S CABIN
Stay in one of the park's 35 cabins, many of which are original Civilian Conservation Corps (CCC) log cabins built in the 1930s. Each cabin is unique, offering a comfortable retreat amidst the natural surroundings.

ATTEND RANGER-LED PROGRAMS
Douthat State Park offers a variety of seasonal ranger-led programs, including guided hikes, educational talks, and moonlit paddles on the lake. These programs provide visitors with deeper insights into the park's ecology and history.

TIPS

- Dress in layers for changing mountain weather
- Visit the Lakeview Campstore and Grill
- 12-month park passports available at discounted rates
- Check schedules for ranger talks and programs

DOUTHAT

BUDGET TRAVEL

WHERE TO STAY
Book one of the park's 35 historic cabins—many built in the 1930s and featuring stone fireplaces and rustic charm—or stay at one of the on-site campgrounds. Sites range from primitive tent pads to electric hookups for RVs, with bathhouses and wooded privacy throughout.

WHAT TO EAT
Bring groceries and make use of the kitchens in the cabins or the fire pits and grills at your campsite—there's a supermarket in nearby Clifton Forge for anything you need. The park's seasonal restaurant offers casual meals with a view of the lake, and the Lakeview Camp Store sells snacks, drinks, and a few grab-and-go items.

SAMPLE ITINERARY
- Friday: Check into a cabin, head to Clifton Forge for groceries and dinner with a pint at Jack Mason's, stargaze by the lake.

- Saturday: Hike the trails, paddle the lake, and relax in the quiet of the park.

- Sunday: Take a morning walk and enjoy coffee before the drive home.

LUXURY TRAVEL

WHERE TO STAY

For a refined stay outside the park, try Ridgely Bed, Breakfast, and Historic Gardens or Hillcrest Mansion Inn in the charming town of Clifton Forge, just 15 minutes away. Those looking to stay within the park can book one of Douthat's renovated 1930s cabins for a cozy, comfortable retreat.

WHAT TO EAT

Pack gourmet groceries to enjoy fireside meals in your cabin, or head into Clifton Forge for provisions. The local supermarket has all the basics, while Mountain Field Market offers artisan goods, fresh produce, and made-to-order sandwiches—perfect for a picnic or an easy dinner back at the park.

SAMPLE ITINERARY

- Friday: Arrive and settle into your cabin with a fireside dinner and stargazing.

- Saturday: Hike the trails, paddle the lake, and picnic along the shore. Unwind with wine and mountain views.

- Sunday: Enjoy a slow breakfast and a final lakeside stroll before heading home.

QUICK TRIPS

SHENANDOAH RIVER

DISTANCE FROM RVA
2 hrs 30 min by car

GEOGRAPHY
Shenandoah Valley, along the South Fork of the Shenandoah River

BEST TIME TO VISIT
Spring wildflowers, summer paddling, fall colors

GENERAL VIBE
Peaceful, relaxing and picturesque; perfect for paddlers, hikers, and families

WHY ITS WORTH THE TRIP

Tucked along the South Fork of the Shenandoah River, this 1,600-acre park offers five miles of river frontage and sweeping views of the Massanutten Mountains. With easy river access, scenic trails, and a laid-back atmosphere, it's a peaceful spot for paddling, hiking, and stargazing by the fire.

EXPLORE MORE

FRONT ROYAL, VA | 15 MIN. N

Known as the "Canoe Capital of Virginia," this small town offers river outfitters, restaurants, a walkable historic downtown, and access to Skyline Drive. Stop by Vibrissa Beer for craft brews, or explore the Warren Heritage Society Museum.

BENTONVILLE, VA | ADJACENT

This quiet rural area borders the park and offers a peaceful setting for scenic drives, horseback riding, and countryside exploring. Stop by local markets, visit working farms, or check for seasonal events like pumpkin patches and Sunflower Days.

LURAY, VA | 20 MIN. S

If you're extending your trip, Luray makes a fun stop with its famous caverns, historic downtown, and scenic trails. Browse local shops, explore the Car and Carriage Caravan Museum, or take a walk along the Hawksbill Greenway.

TIPS

Best reached by car, Shenandoah River State Park's entrance is located just south of Front Royal along Route 340. Parking is available at cabins, campsites, and day-use areas throughout the park. Amenities are limited once inside, so plan ahead and bring everything you'll need for a comfortable visit.

SHENANDOAH RIVER

THINGS TO DO

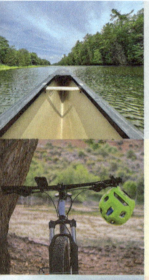

PADDLE OR FLOAT THE RIVER

Canoe, kayak, or tube the South Fork of the Shenandoah, known for its gentle current and mountain views. Local outfitters in Front Royal offer rentals and shuttle services, making it easy to plan a half- or full-day float with convenient access points.

HIKE OR BIKE THE TRAILS

With over 24 miles of trails, the park offers routes for all levels—from flat riverside strolls to rolling woodland loops. Try Big Oak, Redtail Ridge, or Bear Bottom for varied terrain, or combine trails for a longer adventure on foot or bike.

VISIT CULLERS OVERLOOK

This stunning viewpoint near the visitor center delivers panoramic views of the river, valley, and Massanutten Mountains. Accessible by car or a short hike, it's a popular photo stop and a great place to begin or end your day in the park.

TIPS

- Book cabins early—they fill up fast
- Bring river shoes for paddling or wading
- Don't rely on cell service; download maps in advance
- Always wear a life jacket when on the water

THINGS TO DO

GO FISHING OR WILDLIFE WATCHING
Bring your license and cast from the riverbank, boat launch, or quiet coves along the shoreline. The park is also a prime spot for spotting bald eagles, herons, wild turkeys, and deer—especially in the early morning or around dusk.

EXPLORE THE RIVER TRAIL
This wide, flat path follows the river for nearly two miles and connects several key areas of the park. Perfect for a relaxed walk, nature spotting, or photography, with benches and access points along the way for spontaneous riverside stops.

PICNIC WITH A VIEW
Pack your own supplies and claim a table by the river or at one of the scenic picnic shelters. Many areas have fire rings or grills, and sweeping views of the valley or mountains make it easy to stretch a quick meal into a full afternoon.

TIPS

- Use repellent and check for ticks after hikes
- Stay on marked trails and respect wildlife
- Get a fishing license online or at Walmart nearby
- There is a $10 per vehicle park entry fee

SHENADOAH RIVER

BUDGET TRAVEL

WHERE TO STAY

Choose from shaded campsites, heated yurts, or rustic cabins inside the park. Cabins sleep up to six and include basic kitchens, porches, and fire rings, making them a great low-cost option for families or small groups. If you prefer more traditional lodging, check out motels and inns in nearby Front Royal, or browse affordable private cabin rentals in Bentonville and Rileyville.

WHAT TO EAT

Bring your own provisions for campfire meals or picnics with a view Dine out in Front Royal with hearty breakfasts at L'Dees Pancake House, burgers at Spelunker's, or sweet treats from C&C Frozen Treats. You'll also find several budget-friendly local breweries and casual spots along Main Street.

SAMPLE ITINERARY

- Friday: Arrive and settle in. Take a golden hour hike up to Cullers Overlook.

- Saturday: Spend the day on the river, tubing or kayaking. Picnic and unwind at your site by the fire.

- Sunday: Hike a short trail, enjoy coffee with a view, and head home refreshed.

LUXURY TRAVEL

WHERE TO STAY

Opt for a secluded luxury cabin with mountain views, a private hot tub, and upscale amenities—many are just 15–30 minutes from the park. Look for high-end stays in Rileyville or Sperryville, where some cabins include river access, firepits, or even private chefs for a fully tailored retreat.

WHAT TO EAT

Make reservations at Element in Front Royal or Three Blacksmiths in Sperryville for a refined, locally inspired meal—both offer exceptional seasonal menus. Spend a day sipping your way through the countryside's wineries and cideries, or enjoy breakfast and coffee at Main Street Daily Grind before hitting the road.

SAMPLE ITINERARY

- Friday: Check into a riverside cabin and unwind with wine on the deck.

- Saturday: Hike a scenic trail, paddle the river, then savor a chef-prepared dinner or night out nearby.

- Sunday: Grab coffee and a bite in town before a slow drive home.

SECTION 3.

SEASONS & CELEBRATIONS

Not all weekends are created equal—some beg for cozy cabin fires, while others call for cold drinks by the water. The rhythm of the year brings its own charm to each getaway, and timing your trip well can turn a simple escape into something unforgettable.

This section offers inspiration for planning around the seasons, with ideas that pair natural beauty, regional events, and the energy of the moment. From spring wildflower walks and summer festivals to crisp autumn hikes and fireside winter retreats, Virginia shines brightest when the timing is just right.

Here you'll find a seasonal overview to help you plan trips around what nature does best—think fall colors, spring blooms, and summer sunshine.

We've also included a curated calendar of standout festivals and local events happening in or near the destinations featured in this guide. This section will help you make the most of the year's natural and cultural highlights, from timing your trip around a perfect backdrop of fall colors or new flowers, to planning around a special celebration.

FALL FOLIAGE ESCAPES

Fall in Virginia has a rhythm all its own. The air turns crisp, the hillsides light up with color, and small towns buzz with autumn festivals and farmers markets. These are the weekends made for sweaters, cider, and taking the long way home.

Some of the best foliage getaways from Richmond are in the mountains, but you don't have to go far to find a good view. Drive Skyline Drive in Shenandoah National Park, take a walk through Staunton's historic streets, or book a cabin at Douthat State Park, surrounded by golden leaves.

Aim for peak color, usually mid-to-late October, and check local foliage trackers. Early starts can help you avoid the traffic that builds on popular routes.

If you're in the mood for a more active weekend, fall is ideal for hiking, biking, or paddling. Cooler temps and clearer skies make the trails feel different than they do in summer. Try Swift Run Gap on the Appalachian Trail or paddle the Shenandoah River. Fewer bugs, bright leaves, and less heat make it a satisfying way to move through the season. Just don't forget layers because fall weather can shift fast.

COZY WINTER RETREATS

Winter weekends are made for slowing down. The pace lightens, the air sharpens, and quiet corners of Virginia become the perfect backdrop for rest and reset. A snow-dusted cabin in the mountains, a small-town inn with a crackling fire, or a quiet coastal hideaway—this is the season that rewards stillness.

Some of the best cold-weather escapes from Richmond are found in places like Staunton, Luray, or along the wooded edges of Shenandoah National Park. With fewer crowds and lower rates, it's easier to enjoy boutique inns, peaceful trails, and uncrowded downtowns at your own pace.

Pack warm layers and your favorite book, then settle into the slower rhythm of the season. Douthat and Shenandoah River state parks are especially peaceful this time of year, and many inns offer off-season specials that make a quiet retreat even more appealing. Holiday celebrations, candlelight tours, and winter markets bring warmth and charm to even the coldest weekends—check local calendars and plan for a few well-timed surprises.

SPRING GETAWAYS IN BLOOM

Spring in Virginia comes on strong. Wildflowers return to the Blue Ridge, dogwood trees bloom throughout the forests, and small towns start to feel a little livelier. It's a season for stretching your legs, exploring fresh corners, and shaking off the last of the cold.

Charlottesville, Luray, and Williamsburg are especially inviting this time of year. You can stroll through blooming gardens, hike trails edged in wildflowers, or wander through farmers markets and local festivals. Wineries start to buzz again, and historic sites reopen with seasonal events that offer something new, even if you've been before.

With mild weather, manageable crowds, and a full slate of spring happenings, this is one of the best times to hit the road. Many parks and gardens offer bloom calendars or guided tours, making it easy to catch the season at its peak. Whether it's azaleas, apple blossoms, or just a new view you're after, spring weekends offer a welcome change of pace.

SUMMER FUN ON THE WATER

When the heat sets in, it's time to head for the water. A stretch of coastline, a shady riverbank, a quiet lake: summer calls for easy weekend escapes that don't require much more than a tank of gas and a loose plan. Virginia delivers plenty of ways to beat the heat.

Spend a few days in Virginia Beach, paddle the tidal creeks and coastal trails at First Landing State Park, or head inland to canoe a peaceful stretch of the Shenandoah River. At Douthat, you can swim, fish, or just sit lakeside with a book and nowhere to be. Even a short drive can take you to cold mountain streams, spring-fed swimming holes, or shaded park trails that feel a world away.

Pack the cooler, throw a towel in the car, and keep it simple. Summer weekends are better when they're easy—bare feet, cold drinks, open skies, and plenty of time to enjoy them.

LOCAL FESTIVALS & EVENTS

Every destination in this book moves at its own pace—and many mark the seasons with festivals, fairs, and local traditions that are worth planning around. From spring garden shows to fall harvest weekends, these events add something extra to a getaway and give you a clearer sense of place.

It might be a wine tasting in the countryside, a summer concert in the park, or an art walk downtown—whatever the focus, local events often bring towns to life in a way that's hard to catch on an ordinary weekend. They offer a chance to join in, meet people, and see what the community cares about.

This section gives you a month-by-month snapshot of notable events in or near the destinations featured in this guide. It's not a complete calendar—just a short list of happenings that pair well with a weekend away.

Event details can shift year to year, so check local tourism sites for the latest info before you go.

WINTER EVENTS

 DEC | GRAND ILLUMINATION COLONIAL WILLIAMSBURG

Fireworks, candlelight, carolers, and fe
tive cheer in the historic district.

 DEC | CHRISTMAS IN CLIFTON FORGE

Holiday lights, artisan markets, ar
small-town cheer in a charming mour
tain setting full of seasonal spirit.

 JAN | WINTER WINE WEEKEND HARRISONBURG (NEAR A.T. | SWIFT RUN GAP)

A weekend of Virginia wine tastings, pairing dinners, and liv
entertainment at Hotel Madison.

 FEB | WINTER BLUES JAZZ FEST WILLIAMSBURG

A weekend of live jazz performances, wine tastings, and theme
dinners held at venues throughout Williamsburg.

 FEB | FARMERS MARKET – WINTER MARKET WILLIAMSBURG

The farmers market continues through the winter with region:
produce, baked goods, and crafts in a historic setting.

SPRING EVENTS

MAR | VA FESTIVAL OF THE BOOK
CHARLOTTESVILLE

A major literary event featuring authors, panels, and community gatherings throughout the city.

APR | HISTORIC GARDEN WEEK
VARIOUS

Tour private homes and gardens during this statewide celebration of history and horticulture.

APR | TOM TOM FESTIVAL
CHARLOTTESVILLE

Innovation, music, food, and public art take over downtown for a week of spring energy.

MAY | STRAWBERRY FEST AT THE BEACH
VIRGINIA BEACH

Local strawberries, live music, pie-eating contests, and family fun.

MAY | C&O RAILWAY HERITAGE FESTIVAL
CLIFTON FORGE

Celebrate the region's railroading roots with historic trains, model displays, live music, and family-friendly fun.

SUMMER EVENTS

JUNE | JACKALOPE FESTIVAL
VIRGINIA BEACH

A weekend of skateboarding, BMX, and extreme sports, plus live music and beachside fun.

JUNE | RED WING ROOTS
MT. SOLON (NEAR STAUNTON)

A family-friendly celebration of bluegrass, folk, and Americana—complete with hiking, biking, and three days of live music across multiple stages.

JUNE | SHENANDOAH VALLEY MUSIC FESTIVAL
ORKNEY SPRINGS (NEAR LURAY)

Outdoor classical, bluegrass, and pop performances in the foothills of Shenandoah National Park.

JULY | RED, WHITE, AND BOOM
WILLIAMSBURG

Celebrate Independence Day with fireworks, live music, and historic flair in Colonial Williamsburg.

AUG | ART IN THE PARK
STAUNTON

Juried fine art show featuring regional artists, food, and family-friendly fun.

FALL EVENTS

SEPT | PAGE VALLEY WINE FEST
LURAY

Sample local wines, meet winemakers, and enjoy views of the Blue Ridge foothills.

SEPT | MISCHIEF & MAGIC
STAUNTON

Queen City's downtown magically transforms into a wizarding village with themed activities, costumed characters, and live entertainment.

SEPT | ARTS COMMUNITY CELEBRATION
CLIFTON FORGE

Downtown Clifton Forge comes alive with artists, crafters, live music, and hands-on art activities.

OCT | SHENANDOAH FALL FOLIAGE BIKE FESTIVAL
STAUNTON

A scenic cycling event with rides of all levels through colorful mountain back roads.

NOV | VIRGINIA FILM FESTIVAL
CHARLOTTESVILLE

One of the region's top cultural events, featuring screenings, panels, and filmmaker Q&As.

SECTION 4.

PLANNING TOOLS & TRAVEL TIPS

This section brings together your most practical travel tools, designed to help you plan confidently, pack smart, and stay safe—no matter where the weekend takes you. From beach days and time on the water to hiking in one of Virginia's incredible state or national parks, or walking the cobblestone streets of some of the coolest cities on the East Coast, these pages offer the support and straightforward guidance you need to head out with confidence.

Up next, you'll find destination-based packing advice, safety tips tailored to your type of getaway, and a final dose of travel insight to take with you. These tips are here to help you spend less time on logistics and more time enjoying the experience. Think of this section as a quick tune-up for your travel instincts—practical, thoughtful, and shaped by real-world experience.

You don't need a binder full of printouts or a perfectly color-coded plan. Just a little preparation, the right mindset, and a clear sense of what kind of weekend you want. That's what this section is all about.

PACKING FOR YOUR GETAWAY

BEACH & WATER GETAWAYS

Pack light, breathable clothing, sunscreen, a hat, and quick-dry layers. Bring sandals or water shoes, a swimsuit or two, and something comfortable for after the water, like a cover-up or casual outfit. A small daypack, insulated water bottle, and dry bag are smart additions. For boat or kayak activities, include a waterproof phone case and sun-protective gear.

HIKING & PARK GETAWAYS

Choose moisture-wicking clothes, sturdy trail shoes or boots, and a light jacket for changing weather. Pack snacks, a refillable water bottle or hydration pack, and a daypack with room for a map, basic first aid, and extra layers. Don't forget bug spray, sunscreen, and a flashlight or headlamp if you'll be out past sunset.

TOWN & CITY GETAWAYS

Comfortable walking shoes, versatile clothing, and one dressier outfit will serve you well. Bring a small day bag, refillable water bottle, and chargers for your devices. A compact umbrella and light layers help with shifting weather. Visiting historic sites or galleries? A notebook or guidebook can be useful.

STAYING SAFE WHEREVER YOU WANDER

PARKS & REMOTE AREAS

Let someone know your plans before heading out. Cell service can be limited, so download offline maps and save emergency numbers ahead of time. Carry extra water, snacks, and a small first aid kit. Know your route and respect all trail signage. If you're camping, store food properly and follow posted park rules to avoid wildlife encounters.

ON THE WATER

Always wear a life jacket for paddle sports and follow local regulations for watercraft. Be aware of tides, currents, and weather patterns, especially near the coast. Avoid alcohol while boating or swimming, and keep a dry bag with essentials like keys, ID, and a phone in a waterproof case.

TOWN & CITIES

Stay alert in unfamiliar areas, especially at night. Keep valuables out of sight and avoid carrying more cash than you need. Park in well-lit areas and be cautious with rideshares—confirm driver info before getting in. When walking, stay aware of your surroundings and avoid isolated shortcuts after dark.

TRAVEL SMART & STAY CURIOUS

You don't need complicated tools to enjoy a weekend away—just a little planning, a flexible mindset, and a good pair of shoes. You also don't need to travel far to hit the reset button. Some of the best opportunities for rest and reconnection are just down the road. That's a mindset I've come to trust after years of helping everyday people plan meaningful getaways. Use the seasonal ideas and destination tips in this guide as a starting point, then shape your travels around what matters most to you. Hike a new trail, wander through a small-town festival, or find the perfect spot to watch the sunset—let your weekends reflect your curiosity and your pace.

Not every trip has to be big to be meaningful. Some of the best memories come from short drives, spontaneous stops, and slow mornings. Travel isn't about checking boxes—it's about creating space to reconnect, recharge, and rediscover what brings you joy.

So pack light, bring an open mind, and go often. Return to a favorite place or explore somewhere brand new—the goal is simple: get out there, breathe deep, and make it your own.

IMAGE CREDITS

Made in the USA
Las Vegas, NV
05 June 2025

23191313R00066